THE INEXTINGUISHABLE

The Inextinguishable

POEMS

Michael Lavers

UNIVERSITY OF TAMPA PRESS

Manufactured in the United States of America
Printed on acid-free paper ∞
First Edition

On the Cover: West, Benjamin, "Thetis Bringing the Armour to Achilles," 1805, painting, oil on canvas. 2455 mm x 1805 mm. © Photo: Royal Academy of Arts, London. Photographer: Prudence Cuming Associates Limited. Reproduced by permission of Royal Academy of Arts. All rights reserved.

Cover design by Madeline Eisele

The University of Tampa Press
401 West Kennedy Boulevard
Tampa, FL 33606

ISBN 978-1-59732-193-8 (pbk.)
ISBN 978-1-59732-194-5 (hbk.)
ISBN 978-1-59732-195-2 (ebk.)

Library of Congress Control Number: 2023933780

Browse & order online at
utampapress.org

For Claire

Contents

The Inextinguishable

Adonais

Nothing will perish. There is courage.
There are great deeds, and love,
which will last. And the wind,
flipping birch leaves like coins: tarnished bright
tarnished bright. Yes, somewhere
is Verdi and somewhere is Troy.
Claire, Frankfurt before it was bombed is.
It is, and not one thing is taken away,
and Cordelia lives.
Yes, fear and lament. Yes poison
is going into veins from the bag
the nurse has hung. And yet. And yet?
And yet. No pain is permanent.
Those we love will be brought
before us uncorrupted, as they were.
Yes, I believe what I'm saying, no
this is not irony. Wisteria blooms
in that vase on the table. There is
a table. There are chairs, waiting.

A Machine Designed to Hunt Mammoths

Your burden is to make yourself belong here,
though you don't, and in a body where the errors
of the past might see themselves corrected, though misplaced,
misused, shaped by the bog light that designed you,
by the blue deer-haunted mountains, by your thirst, by darkened air
and dappled grass; to hear what you are in the echoes
of hunger, in passing, in the need to go on, to go forward always
on a path kept dormant in your feet, some scent inside
your brain you did not know you were following;
to go through rat-grey water, over hills, over dunes,
under the odors of twilight and the settled stars,
warming yourself by your motion, by the courage
of your going, by glimmers of something enormous
beyond; your burden is to gather everything
as night comes in, to tell the story
of your journey so tomorrow it can start again;
to justify your being here, and then to justify
your imminent going away; to be something
like nothingness, to be even a shadow
of that perfect thing, the thing you are:
the source of an arc, a dangerous edge;
to be a machine designed to hunt mammoths
in the presence of no mammoths; yes, your burden is
to make an end for yourself, a destination
that has been expecting you, which looks at you
the way you always knew you should be looked at,
as a practiced trembling, a flickering fear, a letting go;
to go until the line between you and the world dissolves,
the line between you and what's moving up ahead,
the life beyond your life, ragged and wind-blown,
brooding, vast, hauling its fraying weight
into the future, into nothing, but for now right there,
a lonely flame receding through the snow.

Beauty and Fear

Fair seed-time had my soul, and I grew up
Fostered alike by beauty and by fear ...
　　　　　　　　　　—Wordsworth

I

And then I was: a thing called me. A slight
abbreviation of the air, a clotted wet,

coddled and red. I was the woman wearing white
bent over me, picking us up, the milk's duet,

a hefty, humming rhythm curdling in the dark.
I was the whirlwind of a draining bath, the oozy

coil of kettle-steam, a shadow's arc.
Until I wasn't. One by one things fell away from me,

becoming they: warm lamplight, stars, the screeching
crows, the calm perfected chaos of the cat.

The wind's persuasion showed my shape to me, teaching
me what I was, that this was this, and that was that,

and in between, a chasm, space, insuperable air,
sheer distance that no lullaby could shrink or disavow.

What did I know, huddled in skin? That out there
was the world. That I was here. That it was now.

II

Once mom rolled flat the disc of dough,
she'd let me take the whiskey glass and twist

the biscuits out, a floury archipelago
of coastlines conjured by my wrist

from scraps and straights of yeasty sea,
which she'd ball up, and roll again,

each time tearing away a taste for me,
chin at her elbow, taking in this silent treatise on

the space between us, part and whole,
on how much nothing huddles in the cracks.

Nothing was everywhere: the marble-hungry hole
under the oven, or the drive from Halifax

to Nan's house: hours of blank unbroken snow,
of lightless gaps the night sky brewed,

in which each star sat like a crow
caught in the crowsnest of its solitude.

III

My grandpa held the spoon next to the candlelight.
Showed me my face, but not, warped slantwise

in a wrongness that, who knows, was maybe right,
a bright unmasking of all shape, all size:

my grandma, only crooked, spooning stew
made of potatoes tugged that morning from black rows

and scrubbed so coldly that her hands turned blue.
And then, reflected past her shoulder, windows,

Chevys stretched out snake-like, basking in the sun,
ready to shed their skins, their caked terrain

of Utah, Nova Scotia, and Saskatchewan.
Past them, a smear of cow. Splayed grain.

The truth is what we're used to, just a weave
of light. Now I could really see: the barbed-wire fence

staved like the hymns we'd hum or hold or heave
into the air. The air's immense indifference.

IV

No one knew what it was. No chute for coal,
too cramped for wine, though ageless

vintages of shadow ripened in that hole,
that basement in a basement in the house left to us

by my father's mom, a crumbling Victorian,
complete with secret crypt that let in rain:

a sweaty id hid in its creaking well-bred brain.
Black rats scraped and slobbered in that den,

whose dust and shadows incubated
while I barely breathed, in bed, begging for sleep.

But some mad hag-thing of my making waited,
stewed in the bottom of that fungal deep.

I felt that darkness joined to me, umbilical,
so that if I crept close she'd stir, and blink bright eyes,

burst shrieking from her slimy cell,
and to the top stair, right behind me, rise.

V

It sat mostly unplayed, and yet the whole house
hummed in orbit around that piano's gravity,

that cooling star, whose core arrested us
with molten silence, taut-strung possibility.

I skipped my lessons, slept in, aimed
at lazy mastery of good enough, evasions

as elaborate as the melodies I maimed,
distracted by a new theme, and its variations:

Ann, my teacher. She helped pay for school
by watching me make swampland

of a Schubert *Lied*, or sink into a whirlpool
of dissonance. She'd sometimes lay a chiding hand

on mine, and tease mature, more terrifying tones
out of my fingers, stained still with the mire

of the marsh where I once found, under the stones,
two red newts fused like fierce dark fire.

Filter Queen

Later, of course, I won't believe it.
That what's scattered can be gathered back.
Saved from the swirling eddies of time and decay.
But now? Now Mom opens the door
and shows him in. A heavy man wearing
a red-brown suit. Head sweaty as she brings
him water while her children watch,
certain he would not have faced the heat
without good news. Without the miracle:
he takes it from its case and sets it down.
Pours dirt onto the rug, then waves his wand
and takes the dirt back up, changing
the rug's dull blue to something I did not
know blue could be. From cold dishwater
to a pool of flame. He takes my father's hand
and prints a scarlet O of suction in the skin.
I stare, astonished. Nothing has entered
my life like this. Even an hour later I'll
know better. But for now? Now I believe.
Now Dad's signing a check, proving that those
in charge believe the war on chaos might
be won. The faint smudge of our lives preserved,
atom by atom. The world's frayed loveliness.
Nothing will fade. Mom is alive. One sister's
humming something by Anne Murray, while
the other's playing with two Lipizzaner horses,
which—my God, I had forgotten—she collected.
I remember staring at a row of them
up on her top shelf, thinking, not in words,
Be gentle, Time. Have mercy, Winds. Squinting
through dust-laced air. Seeing their gold hair gleam.

End of the Golden Age

Before today there were no days,
only a cloud, a warm pink haze—
till something shifted. Something cold
now frets the fields with silver mold.
Our hoarded breaths that filled the skies
have fallen down and crystallize
their curse into a shattered glaze,
clenching ripe grass in tarnished greys
and fallen leaves, while our old garden
sees its bulbs and blossoms harden
in a cold-encrusted net
of cabbage steam and crocus sweat.
The crocodiles squint, and crows
laugh at us in our strange new clothes,
while monkeys, whispering, suspect,
suspect: it's our fault things are wrecked,
or slanted slightly, or askew,
and not just out there—in here too,
since thoughts that floated as one mind
now crawl, from me to her, confined
to tongues, to lips, these crude slow trills,
shadowy fragments and loose frills
of what we had, what there should be:
indivisibility.
Where once we wrote on air with flame,
we breathe out smoke; we cry a tame
vapor of vapor, mouthy fumes
whose sweetness sours, disfigures, dooms,
and plain truth lies impearled in these
malevolent embroideries.
This is the end! After a while
maybe the sun will reconcile
leaf to bough, apple to tree,
or something to eternity.

But never us. We stoke small fires
and hope their little heat inspires
some shadow of an older way
that wasn't old just yesterday.

Apollo Considers the Humans

Dear gods, fellow infinities,
let's not debase ourselves.
How many of our countless breaths
are we to waste on such as these?

Consider sea-foam, cave-sweat,
wet snow in a breeze, a low tide's
glittering debris; should we fret
over mere pittances? For wharf rats

drowning in a wave?
Should we let that one there,
inflamed by what's called grief,
dragging his foe through dust,

dazzle eternity? It makes me
dizzy to look so far down.
None of us knows why he
won't join the others eating

squid and roast calf there on the beach
where dusk-fires blaze. Not all
you delegates, not this vast council,
could unravel him to me.

If they know flesh will fail—
spear-torn, despoiled by dogs—then
why anoint it so devotedly in oil?
And in those rare gaps when

they're not driving each other
through, why do they dream
of such dull things: spring weather,
children, or the pinks and limes

of some far city slowly chafed
to nothing by the sea? Sometimes
they make sweet smoke. Some
charms, though dim, shine through,

like when they wash themselves
of blood, pour wine, and waste
the night debating if they're
shade or breath, or more

than eddies of our surplus air,
fleeting as bat-swoop over flame.
Someone says *Yes*. Another *No*.
This lasts till dawn. Not much, I know,

but like fish thrashing in a net,
it's shiny. Vivid. Almost sweet.
The will to bear inside such
small four-chambered stuttering

ten-chambered grief. A wild litany
of pain, and then more pain.
Here only they excel. I've seen
a girl clutching a broken comb

for hours in a strange bed, weeping,
then get up. I can't say how.
Nor why they'll stare all evening
as the sea's roseate darkens to rose,

or smile when their weight
lands on a bent right leg, letting
a javelin go. We are above such
blemishes: the burden of wonder,

or pity, or shame. Risking
nothing for beauty, permitted
no change. Such talks therefore
kill time but settle nothing.

Give them up. Let's leave these
to the bounty of their tears.
Let that one think her husband
still breathes air. Let her, oblivious,

draw him a bath he'll never take.
Let that man, bent by age, driven
by sorrow past all sense, leave
home to beg the body of a son

dragged now through dust for days.
If anything could make me weep,
it would be this, to know his
weeping won't make any difference,

and watch him still go on, foolish
and vain, over the fragrant ash,
down to the ships, down
to the dark undying sea.

Boy with Thunderfoils

He comes, straight from the stables every day,
over the bridge, joining the others walking
winter's blue-mud lanes, slow trickles
pooling at the gates into a crowd.
He crosses through the yard toward the stage,
then goes behind the stage. A flourish,
and a hush, and then he sits. He waits,
motionless, holding the steel tongue of the sky,
muting its cold sharp-edged soliloquy.
Peeking, he sees three thousand faces focused
on one thing, a single action, or a phrase,
what's on the stage, but spilling off, over
the whole vast scale of the seen.
He sees the grief of those whose lives are words.
He sees, sitting beside him on the ground,
the playwright, chin in hand, drawing in dirt,
mouthing the lines. Soon he can tell:
his moment's close, a charge brooding the air.
And there appears, small, like the slit
of a cracked door, glowing in the distance,
in the far crescendos of grief's song, an opening,
a call to shout, to play, to somehow join
the litany, so when the king at last steps out,
screaming and naked, and the boy's whole body shakes,
the sound that comes comes from within,
some faint interior refrain, the pain
of his ten years refracted through these blended
gutturals of fire and steel, the shook-out
sound of heaven, of his self, lamenting
his young life, foiling a king, whipping creation
into doom. A noise of keen delirium,
of faithless air, making the older boys,
dressed up as daughters, flinch. He shakes,
and grown men wail. He quivers, and the whole
globe swoons. Then he collapses, sweating,

hearing nothing, silence and its sweet threat
stopping up his ears. And then at last,
slow baffled sobs. He breathes. He stands.
Exeunt, then home, over the bridge, past dogs
and men sleeping in mud, afraid of nothing
but himself now, of the thing inside of him
no king commands, some mad god
buzzing in his bones, a still awed listening,
faint sobbing everywhere, for all time, without end,
poured out of air, landing on everything.

Self-Portrait

They put him in the car and drove him home,
saying how much he'd love it here.
The sleds they had. Strawberry jam. Pine forests
full of snow that held the twilight's purple shine,
and wolves that stirred the haze over the hills.
They dressed him and applied various creams.
They spoke to him and wanted him to know things:
stories of trolls and fairies. Names for blue.
Where to load the BB and how to aim.
What was Woody Guthrie and what was not.
The woman sitting in bed holding a bowl
and vomiting, saying that if he wanted to cry
he could, him trying not to see, trying to pause
the heart, to force its lastingness, some dark
imperative to be. Then, after, with her gone,
he'd sleep outside, smelling the cinquefoil bloom,
watching his mesh tent sag, heavy with moths.
This is for you, the man said, scraping celery
into a golden broth. Unwrapping cuts
of fish from thick brown paper slowly leaking.
These shouldn't exist, he seemed to mean,
but do. Sleds. Pine forests. Jam. The weight
of something immense coming to rest.
Something they didn't have a name for becoming
something they did. Scraping the fishscales off
and thinking: *Royal. Azure. Powder. Steel.*

Christmas Tree Lights

We have, and then what we have ends.
Is lost, and found, then lost again somehow,
and leaves a kind of stain as recompense,
a smudge which now—

as we sit in the chair by the window
reading Lorca, with the sun on us,
not doing anything—is tinged with sorrow.
It's hard to describe. Except there was,

even on nights like that, a kind of grief,
like the sudden passing of a secret cloud
shrouding the eglantines in a brief
moment of shadow, when their purple bowed

to the thunder in a kind of dialog.
Am I even who I am? Or else was
I, back then, a kind of epilogue
to what's always about to be, but never is?

Those small and intricate evasions of
what exists now only in silhouette, only in speech?
It's like that line from Whitman I love:
It is not far. It is within reach,

which I can hardly get past without tears,
precisely because it *can* feel far, and
whenever we approach, it disappears,
or we do, or there is nowhere to stand

to see it becoming ours, in a way,
in a way that *is* the forgetting,
yesterday and yesterday
and yesterday amounting to nothing

more than this. Which is what?
If everything is farewell, then everything
is also arrival, and maybe we *can* cultivate
a love that knows everything,

even despair. Sometimes all things
seem far away, and in that sense, equal,
and even those anxious evenings—
their dazzling want and sad décor—lose their pull.

I mean those Decembers when, each day
after dinner, Dad would turn on
the Christmas tree lights. I loved the way
they seemed to bruise all being, everyone;

how they arranged and held us all, and how
they brought a million little shadows into play;
how sorrows turn to quiet, tender joys, which now,
held for so long, seemed resigned to stay.

Ode

It started then, having it read to me
by good calm parents who didn't blink.
David dancing naked before the Lord.
I wasn't so young anymore. I'd been
to Michigan. We put a bucket out
and looked at the eclipse in it,
and certain hymns gave me the creeps,
so yeah, I thought, why not?
You kick up dust, you yell and whoop.
You make yourself part of what is,
the one long vowel, lament and ecstasy.
Something like waves, something like
Michigan, where I had been,
but more, the scent of linden trees in bloom,
those long-robed koi, rising slowly,
that would not survive.

      And while it's harder now
to pick out anything but the same thoughts
in new forms, which always used to console,
the ruins of a temple are still holy;
people cross the world to eat
their sandwiches on them and steal flakes
to keep in drawers at home
and show to those they love; yes God
is that which wants the dancing, the naked dancing.
But to live here, in this day? To make
doing the dishes or keeping your hair clean
seem important, and worth doing?
When he was small my son would redo every fall
or stumble a dozen times as if to make himself or us
believe all things were how he'd chosen them,
up down, up down. As if to say: that's me.
Even back then I knew
the choice was to go kicking

and screaming, or go wearing a smile,
saying thank you to the linden trees for being there,
to irises, to grief, to being never satisfied,
which makes us better than the animals.
We like it when the hero dies because
it shows that death can be—must be—
the culmination of a life. The revelation
of what we could be. So that what's left on stage,
untouched by death, we almost feel sad for:
grass, rocks, chorus, fanfare. Silence and tears.
The clouds, the sea.

Your Going

You were going. You were going to go.
Your daughter was driving all night to come see
the mother she knew, but that mother had
already gone. Your husband was going to forbid you
from going but failed. The rain ended
and the sun said *wait*, but you could not wait.
Sorrow propelled you and joy propelled you
to finish your going. To go. To be gone.
To have the day release you from your task
of being here, as your reward for having been.
What could we say of you that would survive?
What last report would give you safety, or
give thanks to those we hoped would salvage you?
I stepped to the window and looked at the pink
evening sky and sipped water and thought
I am drinking! We waited. We ate the cherries you bottled.
We fell to silence or quarrels, but you
were still going, still finding your way.
You wanted to say no but did not know how.
You wanted to say yes but it was being said for you.
The dishes were cleared. The rain stopped.
The rain stopped, the moon rose, shadows
dragged their blue skirts through the corn,
and your going was gone. Then you went,
and the room in your absence grew noisy.
You went with the rest of us already following.
You went, and the world is now only the world.

The Happiest Day of Your Life

You wake up and hear rain. You wake up
and think there's not enough rain, not enough
songs about rain or memories of rain.
Of being numbed or warmed by rain.

You wake up. Your eyes are open.
Lilies in a moss-green bowl. Elms through
the window moving their hands like cellists.
Books exist. And paintings. And pillows.

Blue Mountain and Saddle Mountain.
Abundance Creek. Alpha Centauri. Delft.
The woman in your dream was putting down
a crate of oranges, but then you woke up

remembering there is custard.
There is Verdi, there is smoke-filled
late-fall air. And even joy in what
it feels like to grieve. Wanting to sleep

instead of bear what you must.
Like finishing the best book in the world.
You wake up, wanting to try.
You try. Here in the swirling eddies,

in the dark river of time and decay.
There is rain. There is this day. There is
this day and no other. Praise it with trumpets
and zithers. Praise it however you can.

The Blindness of Homer

Homer is performing at a festival in Colophon. It is the night before his recital begins, and he has come to a sanctuary of Apollo, a simple altar circled by stone markers in a grove on a nearby hill. Hoping to discover why his eyesight is beginning to grow dim, which god has willed it, and what remedy exists, he has brought as an offering a small black goat wearing garlands of pink myrtle. The first drops of blood have barely started to flow when he hears a low voice utter his name.

DAIMON: Greetings, Homer.

HOMER: And to you, Apollo. Tell me if you are truly he, the golden-armed god, that I might praise you.

DAIMON: I am no god, Homer, no haughty immortal. I am your daimon. Or one of your daimons, since there are many of us that compose you.

HOMER: What do you want? Have you come to take this offering intended for a god?

DAIMON: I cannot take anything from you, since to do so would first require that we be separate beings.

HOMER: Then you are an intermediary, come on Apollo's behest to judge my offering? Tell him that this young goat is nothing compared to the gifts I will lavish on him once I return to Chios. My songs have won me many prizes, tripods and gold, shining thoroughbreds and thick wine-colored bulls, all of which I will sacrifice to him if he hears my voice and answers me.

DAIMON: But to see the gods is forbidden, to all except the most elect mortals.

HOMER: Have you not heard of me, Daimon? Or am I not one of
           the elect? Did I not win first honors at the festival at Argos,
           and second place at Mytilene? Was I not an honored guest
           of the widow of Temenus, son of Aristomachus, who gave
           me marvelous gifts, the lyre with a silver cross-bar, stout
           bulls, thick wheels of cheese, and Pramnian wine? Do I
           not excel at singing everything, songs of gods and half-
           gods, of doomed cities and black ships, of those above, on
           bright mist-veiled Olympus, and those who flit in darkness
           down below? What have I left unsung? What more could
           be demanded of a teller of tales? If I am not elect among
           mortals, who is?

DAIMON: I cannot answer that. I only know that some say the songs
           you sing are lies, or at best frivolous distractions, and that
           to recite them is in bad taste, since the singer is so taken
           with his own conceits he weeps and wails and otherwise
           embarrasses himself.

HOMER: Absurd. It is these rumors that are lies, not the songs I sing.

DAIMON: But I myself have seen you, Homer, in the most appalling
           fits of ecstasy, flailing your arms like a man possessed,
           which you are, as I can well attest, but which you would do
           better to conceal. People look at you; they see you talking
           to yourself, or else to me. They suspect that for all their
           sumptuous cadences and fine descriptions, your songs say
           little more than "such-and-such a man was great," or "such-
           and-such a man was killed."

HOMER: What more would you have them say? Besides, even saying
           that much—saying it well, so that it might last forever—is
           immensely difficult.

DAIMON: Forever? Why would you want your songs to last forever? Surely a song which lasts is less beautiful than something like yourself, fated to melt into nothingness. Tell me, Homer, do you sing the same songs everywhere?

HOMER: Yes. I know only the songs my father and mother taught me.

DAIMON: And would you not admit that much depends on those who listen? If they are sleepy or restless, do you not shorten your song, for their benefit, as well as for yours? And if their eyes widen with interest, do you not lengthen your tale, so that they may linger in the most descriptive passages, Achilles dragging Hector's body around Troy's walls, or Odysseus springing like a lion? Would you not draw these out if so inclined?

HOMER: Indeed, I would.

DAIMON: Would you not agree then, that there is no song as such, only these shapes that hint at some other, absent perfection? That your songs are like shadows, which stretch and shorten as they circle around a tree? And that your greatness, such as it is, lies merely in—

HOMER: Enough. I have no interest in such questions. Why can't you simply tell me straight: will I see the face of Apollo, or will I not?

DAIMON: And why are you certain such a being as Apollo exists? Have you ever seen him, or known anyone to have seen or conversed with him?

HOMER: You are infuriating. If I am not to have audience with Apollo, may I put my question to you?

DAIMON: Ask me whatever you wish.

HOMER: Why must I go blind? Already I cannot see half of what I could before.

DAIMON: My dear Homer. The answer is obvious: to increase your inner sight, your insight into men and gods. To ensure that your songs are the best songs. Is that not your wish?

HOMER: What kind of divine gift comes buried in curses? If one of the gods wishes I had keener insight, why not simply bestow it? Why take from me more than what is given?

DAIMON: Why beg to be exempt from what all mortals must suffer? What makes you more deserving of answers or mercy or joy? The gods will not help you, Homer. Nor is it enough to win prizes. You are your own help, and must sing better songs. You must make others see what you are starting to see now: the world not as a war of objects, but a great play of the single light, without division, without end. The way a she-wolf laps up water from a stream, still frothed and bloody from her kill, how flies will hum in summer over pails when milk-foam sloshes over. You must make your songs seem not like songs, but like a river when the sun drapes it in gold. This purpose you have not yet fulfilled.

HOMER: O Daimon, have pity on me. Tell me what I must do to restore my sight?

DAIMON: Have you ever been to Kition, Homer? Have you seen the sheep farmer there, Aëtius? His rams are the biggest in all of Crete.

HOMER: I have not met Aëtius, but that can hardly matter. I have
           known many sheep farmers. As a boy I used to help my
           grandfather with the spring shearings.

DAIMON: Did you not notice how sheep leap about, eat, rest,
           unburdened by worry or thought? How rams chase ewes,
           day after day, never concerned with the past, or anxious
           about the future, never melancholy, never bored, yoked only
           to the moment and its pleasure or displeasure?

HOMER: It is true what you say, and I envy the sheep their oblivion.

DAIMON: In that case, why have you come here? Why have you
           brought this offering? Why do you seek counsel with a god?
           Why, dear Homer, singer of great men, singer of wise men,
           of men who long ago learned how to be brave, why do you
           ask such ignorant questions?

*There is a rustling in the bushes and a boy appears, carrying a jug and a small
bundle of carefully folded cloth. The voice that called itself Daimon disappears.*

BOY: Here's water, Homer, and almonds and a few dates and some
           yellow cheese. [*Stops and looks around*]. Homer, who were
           you talking to?

HOMER: I'm not sure. [*He turns to the boy. The boy approaches him
           and takes Homer's hand*]. A voice claiming to be a daimon
           appeared to me.

BOY: And what did it say? Did it tell you how to keep your sight?

HOMER: No. Or maybe. I'm not sure. You know how puzzling dreams
           can be.

BOY: I do. I had a dream last night that I was big. I was with my
                father, and he started breathing strangely, deep and fast. His
                pipe glowed like a fish, then didn't glow at all. That's how I
                knew that I was big. The first snow was falling, and I was in
                the marsh where I used to catch frogs. Only there were no
                frogs. It sounds sad, but I woke up feeling good, the way I
                did at home when my mother would suddenly turn to me
                and I could tell by her face that I was about to be kissed.
                What do you think this dream means, Homer?

HOMER: How should I know? The gods don't listen to me, and their
                oracles tell me nothing. We are alone, and from the time of
                our first breath, the darkness that's around us only grows. It's
                getting worse. I can barely make out your face, Polydamas.
                You're like a figure drawn in sand, and even in bright light,
                you glow only faintly, like kelp, as I remember, seen some
                evenings on the cliffs of Lindos through a wave.

BOY: Homer, sit down. Let's not get sad tonight. These dates are
                sweet, and the woman who sold them to me said tomorrow
                she'd have plums for cheap, the kind so ripe they're almost
                rotten. I like those the best, dark purple ones, but tinged
                with gold. Let's eat and then let's rest, and in the morning,
                you will say your poem and they will weep just like they
                always do and you will win first place. And if you don't,
                so what? It's a good song. Isn't that true? And isn't it good
                to have known joy, and beauty, even in memories, even in
                dreams?

Pink Clouds

I have the things I want. Another dusk
donning its halo of monotony, wind
noisily existing, the disturbing beauty
of the trees, a moment stretched out
like a landscape that leaves nothing
for the mind to dream up but the small
finesses, minor frills. The aura of anxiety
dissolves, and light, at once ephemeral,
enters the dark enclosures of the heart.
Nothing is hidden. Darkness falls over
the fields like snow, and from my window
I see swallows darting over river-gleam.
The world seems purposeful. Prepared.
More than ideal. It is a mood that lasts
no longer than it's taking to describe,
the consummation of some slow
ecstatic theme. What exactly *is* marriage?
How could the love I feel exist? How,
in the lavish desolation of the years
and stars, could it be merely a digression?
A little smoke. A little shimmering
mirage. Beams of a passing car caress
the wall, Isaak and Magda go on coloring,
and through the window, in the ordinary
sky, pink clouds. Pink clouds. Sometimes
no greater form of joy seems possible.
Sometimes what's best is what is real.

Lines Accompanying the Gift of Four New Strings, Sent from the Mountains of Scythia to a Thracian Musician, B.C. 783

Love, there are tigers here: the dark
will sometimes tighten, smolder, spark
a flickering of motion made
of licking fire, flexing shade,

a sudden wrinkling in the air.
Last night we tracked one to its lair,
and in its foam-flecked throes I heard
a lurking glut of song interred,

so soaked its entrails in a stew
of potash and moon-orchid dew.
I dried the sinews into strings
whose tautnesses and tinglings

were clarified with carob oil
into coil and countercoil,
two treble lines to lift and trace
the throb of bass and double bass,

four strings whose small net can enmesh
the rare advantages of flesh,
or stretch a breath's bright moving-on,
so quickly here, so quickly gone.

I've heard so many lyres played
from Tarsus to Tricominade,
but none has ever broached or bound
such dark conspiracies of sound

like yours. For you chaos supplies
material to organize,
all days, all lives, all things that are
redeemed inside your repertoire:

bones buried under mountain passes,
roiling seas and raveled grasses;
a brightness that your songs exhume
like shark-flash out of undergloom.

A brightness, though, that I won't hear,
stuck on this barbarous frontier.
But distance doesn't make love doubt—
it pulls all of the slackness out,

and though our separation's long,
without it there would be no song:
the strain of so much empty space
tightens our long-delayed embrace,

and makes from our fine-tuned despair
a sweetness, plucked right out of air.

Venice in One Day

I thought a rigid pace
    might coax twelve hours from ten—
eight minutes for the Tintoretto in San Rocco
we might never see again,
        forty, no more, for St. Mark's Square—
but you? You were all loop and linger, stoop and stare,
    soaking your feet in coffee-and-froth-dark waves,

hearing the church bells keeping score
    in San Michele over the graves.
I ran while lunching on a torn baguette,
    pausing for you over the Ponte di Rialto
    and its gondola, like Mesozoic swans,
retracing alleys where our footprints came at us, still wet,
    the tide creeping like calm dark lace.
Lemon verbena at your back climbing a dark pink door.

Where I wanted to be we weren't quite ever yet.
You never had another place to be.
    For you we sat for dinner, and for me
we trailed crumbs of our dessert over the Fondamente Nove,
which I didn't look at and you looked at for too long,
    the sun burning the sea, the sea not burned.

Of course the turns you took were wrong:
    that made them right.
Your circle and my line turned
to a spiral, and the best path was the one we made.
    I finally saw. There was no time.
The church bells stopped keeping their score,
and we were lost. But at your back,

lemon verbena on a dark pink door
signaled the place we started from, and where our bus
began its late-night crawl
                    from Lido to Berlin.
It was a day. It never stopped.
You held the glint of Tintoretto on your skin
        into the future with us,
over the valleys of Neanderthal and Odenthal.

When the Problem Began

How is it that a man can eat his fill
and still feel empty, or that some of us,
with bowls of candied pears, or chocolate mousse
sprinkled with coconut—are so unable
to enjoy our lives, we end them?
It isn't right, we think, to be unhappy
in a chair this soft, gulping the purple
evening air. Here's water, coldly dripping
down the glass carafe; and there a dish
of olives, ripe, though brought to us
from far over the sea. So much abundance,
so much comfort. But so what? Relief
from obstacles becomes an obstacle,
our own thoughts ache, and dawn seems
like a cold star, small and far away.
They just need kids, we imagine someone
whispering, *some people other than themselves*
to focus on, and then they'll understand
what life is for, what love can be. Except,
we do have kids. They came all bruised
and wet and slightly crushed, and seeing
them like that did not solve anything.
In fact, that's when the problem began.

Small Boy Riding a Bike

All day he's scraped himself against
    the edge of skill,
of hard perfection, barely sensed,
    far off. Until

some dark chain finds its gear, and thus
    old skills combine
into an inner calculus
    of weight and line,

of style and turn, of touch and torque.
    Momentum grows.
He's got it now, he's spinning work
    out of repose,

leaning on wind, daring to drift,
    chin elevated,
sure, and not, that this new lift
    is counterweighted

by some ballast in his brain,
    a vast technique
of poise and pitch that must remain
    softly oblique,

unconscious of its own perfection.
    Earth could slip,
but in the casual correction
    of his grip,

be fixed. He is the hub, the gate
    from which the spokes
of wayward stars now radiate;
    now he can coax,

by pumping hard, whatever sweat
    or cadence might
repair the planet's tilt, might set
    the balance right.

All night that sweet, ghostly resistance
    burns his shins.
His mind, now prodigal with distance,
    spins and spins.

On the Anniversary of My Father's Death

Another autumn, so another poem
about how leaves flare into gold and red,
and, fuming, populate the common loam
like the substantial unsubstantial dead.

It's all been said before, how for a while
they fall in single and unhurried file,
then all at once, spreading a brittle hush
over the bee-throng and the squirrel-rush.

Since everything will change but what we say,
say it again: if what we love must mold,
if old limbs must unclench and give away

their lush particulars into the general flame,
we need the leaves next year to look the same.
Their newness dazzles us because it's old.

Low Tide

For six straight days
my bored suburban six-year-old has floated
    in a sun-stroked daze,
      in love with all the lavish frills he's found,
gobbets of flesh the heat has bloated,
    shriveled, blanched, and browned—

    not nereids
sporting in waves, not Venus on her shell,
    but silky worms, dried squids,
      weird scraps of lace the tiderocks hooked and tore,
the cast-off underthings of hell
    strewn on the sandy floor.

    Spent seastars cool
their nether-parts in mud. An eel delves
    through eels. Jellies pool
    and lift their skirts for an anemone
as startled clams unsquirt themselves,
    and urchins shine like money.

    Soon my son's rich
in captives: cockles and chitons stewed in scum,
    that same concoction which
    conspired with a primal sky
and made a sea's unconscious sum
    divide and multiply.

    At dusk, downshore,
we take his pail of temporary pets
    and, kneeling, start to pour
    them out, cucumbers, crablings, snails, this glut
of shells and gauzy silhouettes
    he wants forever. But

we're driving home.
How long could any forms this frail last?
We rinse our hands in foam
and walk back through the woods where shadows grow,
and mayflies flare and dive, who just
last night were embryo.

On Not Having Written King Lear

I don't have to tell you what it's like: you know.
It's just like never having written *Middlemarch*
or walked on the moon. You know that most
people have never written *Middlemarch*
or walked on the moon and yet still get to eat jam
and toast, and stroll with their beloveds
past the cemetery, over the bridge to Main Street.
You know that what you can't do is also worth
celebrating as a source of relief or gratitude,
that love comes only from not being the same
as what you love, that everyone is just one person
and cannot step out of themselves and be
everywhere, as the ponderous afternoon light
that is falling and slightly pink is everywhere.
It's Saturday. So many people have come out
to browse the lonely shops, happy to just look,
to do nothing. But that's something,
just as your beloved promising that this
wrecked wicker armchair can be saved and made
to catch the light again is something: proof
your love is good enough, your masterpiece to see,
to let your dumb-struck silence make things whole.

By the Ships of the Myrmidons

The stirring of the trees had seemed,
just yesterday, dilated with the breath
of paradise. But he had never truly studied
what he was, or what he wanted, which,
right now, was to go home and read,
to inhabit a small room with no view,
far from the sea. Why was it up to him
to help define forever what it means to live?
The mansion of oblivion has many rooms,
and many and vast are the tributaries
of Lethe. What words could he carry
by heart into the reddish hue of the clouds,
words that had not already been written?
How could he ever be of use, do something
to sustain or succor someone through
such general teeming limitless decay?
And even if he could, was that enough?
Soon they'd arrive and beg him back
into his former life. Why not say no?
Why not remain inside some version
of events that will make room for him,
stooped, maybe, but upright, loving what is
bearable to love, playing his little songs
for nobody, breathing the ruinous shade?

Immortality

For many years I had what felt like proof.
The sense of wonder. That I could sob even.
Even in clouds, as clouds, I saw the solace of ritual.
Something like gladness first, until it morphed
into a kind of loneliness or grief.
And even now, at breakfast, the pang
of a call just missed, the need for song,
for rejoicing, for summer winds
like a hand on your back, pushing you on.
Why shouldn't it exist? Here are
yogurt and berries, crêpes and milk.
Smudges of magnitude.
Faint whispers of the soul
of something else. A slow expansiveness
or a complete melting away.
Hunting for graves on San Michele,
or reading Melville in New Mexico;
even just looking up and seeing you
enter the room. Being glad this is my life.
Last week our son, seven years old,
spent all his money on a Chinese water dragon.
When I asked him what its name should be
he just said "Stephen," instantly,
as if things were themselves
and had been forever. Whereas
I think I thought those early hopes
would ripen into joy that was immune
to all the intricate evasions of the beautiful.
I know that doesn't make sense.
But I believed it for a moment, and still almost could.
Things disappear, but are they ever really lost?
I do the dishes, watch the birds move
over the lake, for me the clearest
metaphor for what life is, the luster
of the days I've lost, the flap of distant wings

flying away, then coming back, over
my house, over the hammering next door, over
the music of the men fixing my neighbor's roof.
Songs on the radio that seem too small
to fill the cold blank sky or move these
seamless clouds or fill the leaves back up
with all their tarnished light. And yet
somehow they're not. Somehow they kind of do.
There's something there. The kind of peace
you feel in nothing, in a breeze.
Something like fortitude, or confidence,
some new measure of grace.
I don't have a name for it.
I don't even know it's there.
This is not an argument or an idea.
It's just a feeling, and these days feelings
are all I have. Feelings are everything.

Song for a Severed Head

        … but by the time we neared the top,
I couldn't help it and looked back and saw
she wasn't there. Neither was Hermes.
Only the outer swamps, asimmer with leeches,
only trash heaps and a poison fog roiling the air.
And then those others, mad I didn't love them
with the whole black river of my voice, tore me to pieces,
seeking vengeance maybe for the bruise
of beauty. And my head fell to the river,
where the hollowness of all my thoughts keeps me
afloat. A mad slur gurgling the foam.
Sometimes the rapids hurry down. Sometimes
they level off and show the stars. I float past
towns and ranches, steel mills, silos,
children shrieking, women washing clothes
or mending nets, men hauling scythes back from
a steaming field, doors with nothing
behind them, stairs in the middle of fields
leading nowhere, abandoned cellars where
the moon performs divine ablutions in dark pools.
At night strange fish rise up and suck the air.
Sometimes the glow of cities crowns the hills.
Cows drinking jerk back wide-eyed as I pass,
and then bend down again to brew
their future meals. No one can hear me,
so I sing, not songs so much as
wild delinquencies of sound, and small, since
now each breath falls down, into the dark
ongoing growl of the foam. The world remains
indifferent to my songs, and yet, from this indifference
grows new power, strength past speech,
a magnitude ungraspable, a sound that grows
into its contours and enlarges the circumference
of all breath, all breathable air.
How can one live but in the record of one's loss,

its slow waves lapping at whatever
manages to stay unchanged?
My head is here but I am never where I am.
I live somewhere beyond, a strewn perfection
of which this, the speaking piece, is only one piece,
but implies the whole. The shape
of what forever now their ears will be without.
Already these woods change.
Already I taste salt, some new more vital current,
heavy water surging in, the tang of endlessness
tinging the wind, taking me down to mist, grey light,
high breakers, murky islands, barking seals,
a boundless grey, back out of night,
into infinity. I smile madly
at the sad bright squalor of the world,
the brooding havoc in the clouds, knowing that where
I land, whatever shore, no wanderer will come.
No one will find me, but my songs will last.
Hummed by the trees, locked inside stones …

The Inextinguishable

Son daughter rejoice
they were wrong who said
all things will be taken
that nothing will last
they were wrong

there is no hour of departure
every atom will endure
dust longed to become you
the stars know your names

blue evening light
a window
melon rinds gathering flies
Rousseau's *The Dream*

eons waited for this
small bright true things
saved from the dark

They were wrong
They were wrong
I will see my parents again
what was will be
what is will not change

this table these dishes those flies
rejoice give thanks weep
we go sorrowless
onward forever

Fate

No war to wage, no Sphynx to riddle you,
no whale to hunt. Only the murmur
of the sparrows eating cherries from your grass.
These dust motes floating through this air.
Yes, you are sorrowful. All day
inside the pine boughs it is night,
and no moment is permitted to change,
no beauty to be absent since there is
no absence. No outside, beyond, or above.
Yes, those you have embraced, you are,
and those you have hated you are,
and everything you sing is the song,
the only song there is, the song of these stones,
picked by your daughter from that hill.
Waiting these eons for their Orpheus.
To be rescued from oblivion and held aloft.
There is only one road and you are on it
and you live with the gods and the cacti
are flowering. Here by the window,
where your wife is giving them their
little slurp of monthly rain.
Of course you are sorrowful.
You must be to see that the song gets sung.
To approve, of the whole thing, over and over.
To watch the sparrows fly up to their branch
and say to them: *stay where you are.*
To look up at the stars and think: *do that again.*

Chaos Soliloquy

Not what they think I am, these creatures
on the bus: not just the shoeless man
slumped in the back, or tents under
the overpass on Seaview Road: a mere
gazillionth of the whole of me, bolus
of ocelots and astral gasses and bent light.
This woman in the mauve dress doesn't know
I haunt the organ score she holds as freely
as I fill her grandson's headphones,
noise like Visigoths ransacking Rome.
That man in coat and tie? I am that coat
and tie, and I'm what spiked his email
with a typo that had students rummaging
for clues about the whiteness of the whale
in chapter 4, instead of 42. I led him
to his wife, and her into her migraine's
third straight week. Those sirens? Rubble? Traffic?
Shattered glass? Me, me, me, me. But then
there's broom me, stretcher me, bright floppy
body me, being revived. Just look around:
all this was sea once, then a mountain,
now there's Jamba Juices everywhere!
And far past them, something called Mexico.
You're welcome! Still, the organist
would banish me, and hopes her grandson
will exchange the clamor of smashed temples
for the hum of Luther's harmonies.
But why? I midwife all she loves. I am
the dissonance that makes the mighty fortress
of her song so sweet, a bulwark from my barbarous
and silent shadows, endless cold, thick mist.
Nor will the teacher ever feel the sunlight
like his wife will when the migraine lifts:
not as a curse, but as a cure,
a consolation lavish and complete.

Isn't it great? Me cells quadrupling.
Me sculptor of luminous noise. Me hullabaloo.
I wander lonely as a universe,
I'm everything, all matter and all time,
all lesser scrapes and major spills, rumor
and fact, structure and strife, the smallest
tributaries and their sum, the sea;
I'm all the joyous weeping of the world,
and from my everything, some sudden spark
might come, some unplanned sense, some happy turn:
Woman Holding a Balance by Vermeer.
Snow falling on moving water.
Heorogar, Hrothgar, and Halga the Good.
Today the teacher woke to find his dead lawn
purpled with the petals of his neighbor's trees.
Kudos to me. Could be that chapter 4,
with Ishmael and Queequeg snuggled up,
the leg of one flopped tenderly over
the other in the cold New Bedford dawn,
contains the true key to the whale's hue.
Maybe his students, sacks of mostly
water still, still might become what he
has always wanted them to be: little
grenades of joy books are the fuses to,
swooning and dazed, finding texts everywhere—
the most inspired readers in the world.

Three Buttered Muffins

Mr. ———, who loved buttered muffins, but durst not eat them
because they disagreed with his stomach, resolved to shoot himself;
and then he eat three buttered muffins for breakfast, before shooting
himself, knowing that he should not be troubled with indigestion.
—Boswell

I want to ask poor Mr. ——— why, if life's
so bad, he paused to savor them at all? But I
know why. How could the scent that spirals
up the stairs *not* sway him, for the moment,
to put down the gun, and come, and break
a muffin open, watch the steam spill out?
To wedge fresh butter in each porous hinge?
To want, for once, to live one moment longer:
there are muffins, after all. And here is butter
catching candle-light, sighing its soft glissando
down the spongy muffin-flesh, hinting
that joy, though soft and all too solvent, still
anoints some moments with its glossy smear:
joy in the mint-flecked ruminations of the cow
at milking time, the greasy fingers of the girl
who sets her pail of white froth down and lies
under the ilex boughs and weeps over some boy,
then in a minute gets back up, and wipes
her cheeks, shakes out her thatch-flecked hair;
not that she knows some pleasure's only felt
because it ends, that it cannot be held, raised up
like curds of butter that her mother calls forth
from the churning chaos like fermented light.
Not that. She just remembers there are muffins
waiting for her, too, back in the house, and when
they're gone, maybe some milk. Maybe an apple.
Maybe, since it's not impossible, some cheese.

From the Museum of Failed Masters

Here you will feel no ecstasy, no bright
imperative to weep, or to give thanks,
or to endure. Instead, we offer solace
in what's gaudy, saccharine, timid, tame:
in trees rigidly perfect, Christs with too-white
teeth, a sunset blushing at its own excess.
The portraits here preserve the blind precision
of the novice, those who kept on polishing
long after likeness came, whose paintings lack
the cracks that signal life, the flaws
that prove vitality, that capture change.
We honor those who stayed inside the margins
of their skill, too satisfied with what they
understood, choosing a mild perfection
over jagged honesty, a safeness glazed
to an intolerable glow. Nothing will
crush you here, nothing seems far away.
So come. Enjoy an ok sandwich in the atrium.
Stay for the day. Come celebrate those brave
enough to spotlight their timidity,
who make the world you'll walk back into—
with its mildewed leaves and crooked teeth—
feel right: the glow of nothing much
on everything, the dull grey sky worth seeing,
faces easy to stare at with their faded shine.

A Minor Scribe Defends His Diction

It's true I may have overstepped by adding "very"
to the part where God, judging his handiwork,
pronounces it not only good, but very good,
seeing the whole. But since we're turning
tales made out of breath to writing—
something solid, and, who knows, maybe
enduring—I thought: why not polish this
or that small flaw along the way? I'm hoping
that as head of this committee, you'll agree.

The balance, you'll admit, is delicate:
a word like "perfect" wouldn't hold: too many
little graves, too many dried-up wells.
But simply "good" feels spare, too scanty
for a world where there are grapes and almonds,
hair and faces, wind-combed grass, those birds
I've seen out west with bright blood-colored wings.

No, "very" sets our readers' expectations right,
a word neither too coy in its critique
nor cloying in its praise, right for a world
where hope at least is possible, where somewhere
better is forever over the horizon
and worth setting off towards, a line of oxen
hauling our possessions through the hills.
What do we love God for if not this balance,
showing us the middle road: not just one
type of maple, or a showy million,
but a fair one-twenty-eight, pushing
himself to *sugar, downy, fullmoon, jade.*

When you consider, Chief Scribe, that there's
not only an absence of oblivion, but me, somebody
in his forty-seventh year granted an evening
by threshed corn, smelling the dusk-bruised dirt,
I'm sure you'll see my small insertion isn't
merely a description of creation, but
a vital part of it, creation smiling on itself.
Sometimes bright clumps of berries shine.
Sometimes your tongue will taste for hours
like the lips of one you love, a taste no pain
of parting and no wine can wash away.

And even with the fresh stains on your hands
from digging one of those small graves, it's not
impossible, as I well know, to think
creation's first six days still merit praise,
that God deserves the savor of our smoke.
When my surviving son stands back and tilts his head
to judge the full scope of a sketch he's made
then crouches down again to fix some flaw,
I know why God needed a seventh: not to rest,
but to lean back and assess—the rightness
of peach down, tree frogs, yellow finches,
and the wrongness of our sloth or rage.

And if God is a potter, as some early tales
suggest, I'm sure this Earth, not highly, hugely,
or extremely good, would still be good enough
to show off to the other gods at festivals,
and not a dud he'd grind back down to clay.
Of any ten pots, say, how many outshine Earth?
Today, when air is gritty, but the light shines
sea-green from the coast, my guess is two.
Or three. Or maybe four. Four at the most.

The Happiest Day of Your Life

If it must be like this
if we must be reminded the body is frail
if the body is frail
if my children must weep over nothing
a torn foil sword
or a lost cardboard shield
and since chaos so often wins
let's demand what we can
let it grant us at least for a moment
the world
let me once
make my daughter's braid tight
let the pear branches bow
to the weight of their fruit
and let bread dough defy disarray
let these stamps be put on those envelopes
the body is here
let it want to be here
let its knowledge not bow to the mind's
that the future is dark
let me read to the end
but read greatly
and so the Trojans buried Hector, tamer of horses
let our gift to tomorrow
be thinking instead of today
where my son shows his sister to tape up her sword
how to wave it in rage at the air
no go higher like this go like this

The Cacti

Then, to my safe dull world, they came,
weird birds my wife wanted to tame,
legions of spikes and spines and quills
roosting on tables, crowding sills,
maces and morning stars that she
rifled from nature's armory,
half-sprung grenades and razor gauze
filling the gaps where softness was.

Brought home from nurseries, shipped by mail,
two inchlings culled from roadside shale
illegally, three filling shelves
with inbred cuttings of themselves,
crude cousins in a hunchbacked bloom
colluding across the living room.
Here dragon eggs, there devil's phlegm,
a barb-encrusted diadem

of torturous gold, tantrums of green:
why are they here? What do they mean?
She dotes and fawns, but can't appease
their anti-social tendencies,
and so a dust of spidery hairs
(despite the doubled gloves she wears)
will keep her scratching where they kissed
a bared knuckle, an exposed wrist.

If nature doesn't make mistakes,
then what are these? And yet she makes
more space for them, until our mild
safe house has grown carefully wild
with ragged stalks and snarling ropes.
She's right. Somehow these misanthropes,
these gargoyles, barbed and hairy,
sharpen the need for sanctuary,

and are proof that paradise
is fenced by ugliness and vice.
Even perfection needs its flaws,
the thrill of risk, the threat of claws.
Why be so picky with my praise?
Turning the lamps off, she surveys
a world of troll, pagan, and infidel
grinning in moonlight. All is well.

So Far Away Now I Can Almost See It

The field was thus, the bread was so.
Birds lifted over the bay and seemed.
Gulls hissing loudly as. A grey light
turning into, or waves unlike anything in.
Or a forgotten dream of, only more so.
I.e., thick fog creeping through the grass
recalled to mind. Recalled to mind the.
Train and river, drunkards and tramps,
the sea being the sea. I.e., night and roses.
Schubert sung out of an open window.
Quail eggs, rhubarb, moon-white cliffs.
Cappella Palatina and the sense that something
any minute might. That sparrows would.
Palermo, 3 AM: how to describe it?
Or your mouth—the peril of. And frescoes.
Then that dog, barking like noise would
keep the flocks of stars in place. Of course
it does. The silence, thunder. Silence,
silence. Silence, rain. You holding me.
You holding me was like. Was almost like.

Sun, Birds, and Leaves

Sun, birds, and leaves, outside my window.
Sun, and birds, and leaves, and a valley,
and a lake, and beyond that, hills. The sun
that is on me. The birds that are birds.
Small wings and frail backs. Sparrows
bobbing in a cold wind on the wheat stalks
near the fence, perched sideways, hanging on,
some nearly upside down, tearing off seeds.
Yes, I watched my mother die. She moaned
until she had no voice to moan but was still
in pain, and I have not forgotten. The seizure
in the bathtub, getting in with her
and holding her up so she did not drown.
Who's to say things should be different?
It is spring and there are birds, and sun,
and leaves, and my happiness in this moment
knows death. It has agreed to the moaning.
It seeks neither recompense nor relief.
Heaven is here, and I have not forgotten.
I smile because I want to, knowing.
I stare and stare. I ask nothing to change.

The Happiest Day of Your Life

You buy a cat for your children.
You hang that print of Vermeer, a woman
in blue reading a letter.
You breathe the air, shoveling snow
clotted with cherries off the curb
as black crows call out "Death,
Death." But the cherries are limitless,
and the world wants nothing
but the endurance of its journey.
To be born anew each moment
inside you, who can never die.
You who will save the world.

Ode to Ignorance

To dark. To that kingdom of plenty.
To Homer's mother cutting squid.
Tying her hair up as her boy comes in
in tears. I'm chasing the other boys, he says,
but things are dark. I trip now. I fall down.
To Keats not being able to read Greek,
and to this garden's jasmine: what is jasmine?
And to how there's always more to know
about the woman at the garden's other end,
weeding the pumpkins. To our children,
chasing dandelion fuzz across the yard,
spooked by the bees brawling for windfall pears.
Above, an airplane scrawls a one-line ode
to knowledge, which deserves my praise.
Just not right now. Now it is morning.
Gnats dance, and blue finches sing.
Rose petals pirouette through morning air.
To how not even Keats knew how he wrote his odes.
To how what Fanny really thought of them,
down in the smoky rivers of her heart,
maybe he didn't want to know,
and to the days before I knew: nothing comes back,
not pears to their boughs, not gnats to their eggs.
Not the piece of me that is in you, over there,
weeding the pumpkins. Because I saw our kids
arrive head first, top heavy. And because
the blind boy's mother made him practice
wading through the dark, just to the tree line first,
then in. Into the rhythms of his mind. Into
that deathless company keeping the citadel.
Into a whole new kind of song.

Last Night's Snow

My lord, wake up. There's snow. It fell all night.
Snow on the inns and taverns, hovels, lanes;
on courtyards, alehouses, guildhalls, gates.
Look at the baker's son, dropping his loaves
on ice; the harlots huddled on Hog Lane.
Moorgate and Cripplegate covered in snow,
the palace lost inside the commonness
of snow, all London hushed like under lamb-skin:
snow on posts and pillories and stocks.
On the unburied dead. On ancient graves.

Wake up, my lord. Here's cheese, here's ale,
and your long pants, and your boots, unpolished,
as you like. Look how the sky seems lighter,
like a ship back from the land of spice,
unburdened of its load, the whole world packed
in salt, the beef-stalls and the breweries,
the herring smells and onion smells, the smells
of ague, pox, and plague smothered in snow,
which, like yourself these days, is not itself,
but lays there, still, and takes its form from all
it touches: soldiers, courtiers, vagrants, strays.

Why not get up and start something, some
monologue, some scene? Let me be in it,
as a servant, and your boy—what was his name?
You know the plague took mine away, those mocks
and gibes that made his mother roar, all gone,
melting like snow into eternity. But sir, to live
is to endure such things. To let things be.
Why not give yours some speech, some shape?
Make him a prince. Say that we shall not die,
but shall be changed, that man's a wondrous
animal, a thinking dust, a radiant thing.

My lord, here's ink. Here's paper. Look sir.
Master Shakespeare. Will: do you not see?
It is for you all this is happening,
St. Paul's and Bishopsgate covered in ice,
the whole smashed glass of cloud and sky;
the highwaymen and hangmen, mongers, hawkers,
nobles, waifs, the shivering laundresses
and limping smiths, the carts and carriages
on endless show; for you their entrances
and exits; this absurd bright air and all
it touches. All these people. All this snow.

Autumn Evening

Scrub jays, out the window. Wild mustard.
Road. Mountain. Watering can.
A day to abandon expression since what can be expressed?
Not darkness, or the early calm over the fields.
Not Claire roasting garlic and tarragon in oil.
Not candlelight. High, wavering.
Not the lake ice of my boyhood, part pink, part blue.
Coming to me now, unbidden, as if to console.
Console for what? I asked for words
to become a life, and they did. Here I am.
One of the lucky to whom the Earth was offered.
I asked for awe, and ordinariness flared:
road and mountain and watering can.
The persistence of grief as a source of delight.
My belief in the soul, which I cannot believe.
Candlelight, high, wavering.

Legacy

after Goethe

Nothing can fall to nothing.
Things change, but remain, pushing
us on, making us happy to just be here:
clouds or rain, two cardinals on a bough;
the smell of the sea suddenly everywhere;
the high gloss of what is, right now.

What's new today is old, and always was:
compost of petals and overripe plums,
the glint of the sun on the tiled roof,
a new recording of the cello suite you love.
What saves us is our awe, knowing the sum
of all that's beautiful was made for us,

folding our children's clothes,
watching the bruise of evening clot the air.
What else are we for? How should we measure
ourselves? Where is that version
of our lives in which all paths compose
the main path, where nothing is a digression,

no matter how small? What do we actually
see, smell, feel? The music of our thoughts
keeps us alert, and won't deceive us as we
stand up, move around, construct, or try,
our own way through the one way
that there is, the meadow-studded world.

Wherever it is, you can get there. It doesn't take
much when each scrap hoards an eternity:
some eggs, kids throwing rocks into a lake,
tables and chairs, the curt blue whisper
of a lighted match, a bucket clanking
at your knee; until, eventually,

in the end, steeped in the certainty
that what's true never dies—like grass under
the snow, still simmering light, still green—
we'll worship what we have, the mystery
of clean white napkins, cows in mist,
an orange loosened from its darkling tree,

till, quietly, like always, like before,
like all the masterpieces we adore
for following no rule or impulse but their
own hidden momentum, we'll be what we love.
We'll have become what we are.
We'll have discovered how to live.

Acknowledgements

To Claire Åkebrand, inexpressible gratitude.

I would also like to thank Malachi Black, Scott Hatch, Susan Elizabeth Howe, Lance Larsen, Jacqueline Osherow, John Talbot, and Claire Wahmanholm.

Grateful acknowledgement is made to editors of journals in which some of these poems first appeared:

32 Poems	"Venice in One Day"
	"The Cacti"
AGNI	"A Machine Designed to Hunt Mammoths"
AGNI Online	"Last Night's Snow"
Blackbird	"Song for a Severed Head"
	"Apollo Considers the Humans"
	"Adonais"
The Bombay Review	"On Not Having Written *King Lear*"
BYU Studies	"The Happiest Day of Your Life"
The Gettysburg Review	"So Far Away Now I Can Almost See It"
The Hudson Review	"Beauty and Fear"
New Ohio Review	"Three Buttered Muffins"
Ploughshares	"From the Museum of Failed Masters"

"Chaos Soliloquy" won the 2021 Moth Poetry Prize.

"Low Tide" won the 2020 Bridport Poetry Prize.

"Filter Queen" won second place in the 2020 Troubadour International Poetry Prize.

"Boy with Thunderfoils" was shortlisted for the 2020 Montreal International Poetry Prize.

"Ode to Ignorance" received honorary mention in the 2021 Fish Poetry Prize.

About the Author

Michael Lavers is the author of *After Earth*, published by the University of Tampa Press. His poems have appeared in *Ploughshares*, *AGNI*, *Southwest Review*, *Best New Poets 2015*, *TriQuarterly*, *The Georgia Review*, and elsewhere. He has been awarded the University of Canberra Vice-Chancellor's International Poetry Prize, the Moth Poetry Prize, and the Bridport Poetry Prize. Together with his wife, the writer and artist Claire Åkebrand, and their two children, he lives in Provo, Utah, and teaches at Brigham Young University.

About the Book

The Inextinguishable is set in Garamond Premier Pro digital fonts, based on orginal metal types by Claude Garamond and Robert Granjon that were designed and cast in Paris, France, in the sixteenth century. The book was designed and typeset by Wesley Kapp at the University of Tampa Press.

Made in United States
Troutdale, OR
02/17/2024

17681129R00051